MW01172251

Affirmations from

The Goddess Tribe

RADIANCE SATTERFIELD

For Claire and Sky

Name: Satterfield, Radiance
Title: Affirmations from the Goddess Tribe / Radiance Satterfield
Description: [Pompano Beach, Florida] : Aqua Creative Marketing, [2019] | Series: The Goddess Tribe; [2]
Identifiers: ISBN-13: 978-1-7323507-3-1 (paperback)
Subjects: LCSH: Spirituality | Self-help | Prayer

Paperback: ISBN-13: 978-1-7323507-3-1

You are free to make your own mistakes, to live as you choose. You are free to live in Faith and Understanding. You are the creator of your own life. You are free to live passionately. You paint the pictures of your life. No one has the power to fix you, to heal you, or to hurt you. You are Spirit. You are light. You have the power, in your own way, in your little corner of the world, to create heaven on Earth.

~Radiance Satterfield, The Goddess Tribe

Contents

7

Introduction

After writing my first novel, The Goddess Tribe, I began leading workshops and retreats based on the book. Invariably, at these engagements, readers, friends, and fans would happily inform me of a little trick that they had developed. Several had copied down all the affirmative prayers from The Goddess Tribe novel and were carrying them around in a specially decorated Goddess Tribe journal or notebook.

This handy volume could then be referenced any time during the day or night, as needed. Whether waiting at the doctor's office, the DMV, or quietly sipping coffee at her favorite café, women were taking their prayers with them. Nothing could have pleased me more! And while I was truly delighted that my affirmations were enjoyed even beyond the story of The Goddess Tribe; with only twelve, I knew what I had to do. Encouraged by enthusiastic readers who were asking me for more, I suddenly felt the pull to write a full volume of affirmative prayers. I tried my best to cover most areas of life for which we commonly need prayer. For me, this is pretty much every circumstance that life throws at me, from feeling shy and lonely, to feeling incredibly bold; from grief to joy. Yep, as I like to say, I have an affirmation for that.

What is an affirmative prayer? The answer is this: An affirmative prayer is a way of speaking to Divine Source with intention rather than with begging or beseeching. I believe that Spirit is everywhere which means that Spirit also dwells within you, me, and everyone. In affirmative prayer, you state your truth and your intention in the present tense. For example, "I am Love" is an affirmation. Whereas "Dear God, please send me someone to love!" is begging rather than affirming. Here, you will find the original twelve affirmative prayers from the much-loved novel, The Goddess Tribe, along with many more to touch your heart.

I have, as with The Goddess Tribe a novel, poured my heart, soul, time, and treasure into this little book. After completing The Goddess Tribe, I had an experience that may be called a near death or out of body experience. I had little time to process what happened before publishing, working, and touring for The Goddess Tribe. I had no time to grieve or make sense of what had happened to me. I decided recently to begin speaking about my experience. The more I share it, the more exposed I feel. More and more pain floats to the surface. As I now have finished writing Affirmations from The Goddess Tribe, I can honestly say that this work has been my pleasure. And it has been my therapist, pastor, sister, and partner. My sincere hope is that reading these prayers feeds your soul as much as writing it has fed mine.

Namaste,

Radiance

Faith

We are the presence of Pure Being,

The Sisters of the Goddess Tribe.

We affirm that Goddess Power lives within us,

Flows through each of us,

Connects us all to each other, to our world,

To our universe.

Thoughts such as lack, fear, hatred, and poverty

Have no power over us

For they are just thoughts.

We live in joy, abundance, and prosperity.

Every day it is ours to claim.

And we are grateful in this knowledge.

And so it is.

Amen.

13

Strength

"Today we invoke the two most powerful words in the Universe. I Am. Thousands of years ago, the ancient Hebrews' name for God was Yahweh, which translates to 'I Am,' meaning that God dwells within. Jesus knew this as he proudly claimed the words, 'I Am,' striking jealousy and fear in the hearts of the Pharisees. And we too, Ladies of The Goddess Tribe, shall call forth the Power of affirming 'I Am', as The Goddess dwells within." ~ Maymie

I am the Power of Strength

Which dwells within my soul.

I release the false beliefs from my heart

Which separate me from Oneness.

I embrace The Goddess Power of Strength

Which holds me steadfast, strong, and sure.

I am The Goddess who stands firm in my Strength.

I am The Strength which guides my destiny and Claims

my voice.

14

I am The Mother who proudly protects all children.

I am The Goddess who shields the meek.

I Boldly walk the path of peace.

And for this I am so grateful, and I say Thank You.

Amen.

Wisdom and Judgment

I am Divine Wisdom,

Expressed in my thoughts, my words, and my actions.

I am Divine Judgment,

Carefully weighing the consequences of my behavior.

I am the Goddess Sophia,

Keeper of the Old Knowledge.

Jealousy, foolishness, and strife do not enter my life.

I am Queen of Wisdom.

I willingly shine my light to others who come to me

For prayer and advice.

I feel Divine Wisdom flowing through me like a river.

I lovingly pour my Wisdom onto the world.

And for this I am grateful.

Amen.

Love

Today, I affirm that Divine Love is all around us.

Divine Love dwells inside all beings,

Connecting us all in oneness.

There is no separation, no fear, and no strife.

For all creation is Love.

And all Love is creation.

Anything else is an idea

That we have the power to deny.

Love lives in us and works through us at all times.

And for this, we are so grateful.

And we give thanks.

Amen.

17

Power

I am the Goddess in expression,

Creating my life with my very thoughts.

I am the Universe becoming self-aware,

Start-Dust, Magic, and Infinite Power.

I am the Power of Love,

Spreading my arms around the Earth.

Bringing Love where there is Hate,

Hope where there is fear.

As I join my sisters in Goddess Mind,

Our collective thought has the

Power to change the World.

Knowing this Power,

I keep my thoughts pure,

Centered in Love at all times.

I reject ideas involving fear and hate,

Embracing only Love and my Infinite Power

To make the world a better place.

And so, it is.

Amen.

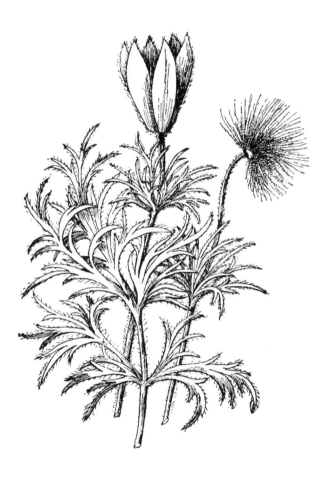

Imagination

I am The Goddess Power of Imagination.

Divine Spirit dwells within me,

Blessing me with a boundless ability

To visualize all good.

With my strong Faith, I open my mind to

Visualize the world as it should be,

A world filled with Peace, Love, Prosperity,

And the birthing of Divine Ideas.

I reject all thoughts of hate, fear, and lack.

For these thoughts do not serve me.

They do not serve our world.

Instead I focus my Goddess Energy

On all that is good.

I use my imagination to see my world ruled by the

Power of Love,

And for this I am grateful.

Amen.

Understanding

Today I affirm Divine Understanding.

Together in Divine Understanding we see

The Goddess within each of us

We see

The Divine being sitting next to us

I AM

The Divine being sitting next to you.

I understand and know

The Goddess Spirit is inside me

Is a part of me,

Is me.

Is you.

There is no separation.

Only oneness.

Through Divine Understanding

I receive Divine Inspiration

I know my purpose.

I know what I must do.

And for this I am so grateful.

And so it is.

Amen.

Will

I am the power of Will

Using my talents for the greater good,

Following my divine calling.

Through prayer, I discern the best path to follow

As I reach understanding in my mind, body, and spirit,

My power of will propels me toward my divine

purpose

With good judgment, zeal, and imagination,

I boldly take steps to become the person I am meant

to be

I powerfully claim all that is mine to do

And I follow my spiritual path in grace and

steadfastness.

For inner knowing, I am grateful.

And so it is.

Amen.

Divine Law

I am Divine Law

Invoking the powers of

Judgment and Understanding

In order to identify Divine Inspiration.

Through prayer and meditation,

I receive my calling.

Through Divine Will, I remain steadfast,

Acting on Divine Inspiration.

According to Divine Law,

I must do what I am called to do.

When I act in accordance with Divine Law,

I live in Joy, Abundance, and Love.

If I act against Divine Law,

I struggle.

I suffer.

And I wage an uphill battle against myself.

With this Great Knowing,

I forge ahead joyfully heeding my call,

And living life according to Divine Law.

For this, I am grateful.

And so it is.

Amen.

Passion

The Power of Divine Passion flows through me,

Igniting my creativity, self-expression, and courage.

I thirst to express myself in Zeal.

Joyfully, I follow my spiritual path with enthusiasm

Denying the power of

Abdication,

Self-doubt,

Mediocrity,

And Conformity.

With much gratitude, I steadfastly pursue my Divine

Calling.

Thank you, Sweet Spirit.

And so it is.

Amen.

Release

I am the Power of Release

I am Renunciation, Elimination, and Purification

I breathe out anger, resentment, sorrow, and fear

I breathe in joy,

Acceptance, contentment, and strength

I Release thoughts, beliefs, ideas,

Stories, and memories

That no longer serve my highest self.

In so doing I cleanse and purify

My body temple and my soul.

For this, I am grateful.

And so it is.

Amen.

Life

I Am the Power of Life,

Joyfully experiencing all of the good

That the universe offers me.

I Am health, vitality, and wholeness.

I Am joy, exuberance, and glee.

I delight in all of the beautiful gifts of my world.

Ideas such as illness, pain, and lethargy

Have no power over me.

For I am filled with the Spirit of Divinity.

And I express Divine Life every day

And in every joyful way.

I am forever in gratitude for

My body, mind, and spirt.

Thank You. Thank You. Thank You.

And so it is.

Amen.

Elimination

I affirm that I am one with all

One with Divine Spirit.

And that I have everything that I need

Within me.

With the power of elimination,

I let go of old ideas and beliefs

That no longer serve me.

I let go of old clothes, old household items,

And old memories

That I have outgrown, in my journey of expansion.

I need not hang on to a past that is behind me.

Ideas such as fear, separation, and isolation

Have no power over me.

For I embrace my Divine Oneness

With all that exists.

I am grateful for this understanding.

And so it is.

Amen.

Grief

I affirm that grief is a natural part of life.

I have the right to grieve.

I owe it to myself to take time to grieve.

I have experienced loss.

I feel sadness.

And that is alright.

I do not hide my grief to spare others.

I do not pretend that everything is ok.

I feel sadness.

I am experiencing sadness.

I am working through this journey of sadness.

This is my journey.

No one else's.

When I am finished grieving,

The sun will come out again,

And I will rejoice once more.

33

But for now,

I continue my journey though grief.

If I need help,

I ask.

If I feel I cannot go on,

I ask.

When I need support, I ask.

Knowing that Divine Spirit is here with me

At all times,

Knowing that the Soul is eternal,

And that loved ones too, are eternal,

I affirm my right to grieve.

And so it is.

Amen.

Forgiveness

I affirm the Power to Forgive and Release

Negative people and negative energies

From my journey.

Realizing that we all make mistakes

And we each have a unique story,

Which may include pain and fear.

Which may include loneliness,

Heartbreak and anguish.

I send love and prayers to those who have hurt me.

I release all bad feelings to the wind.

I do this daily if I need to.

I release until they are indeed,

All gone.

For I know in my heart,

That holding on to anger, hate, pain, and fear

Will make me sick.

I walk away lighter, happier;

Shining my light brighter than before.

And so it is.

Amen.

Prosperity

I affirm my Power of Faith

In my ability to manifest

The Prosperity that I want in my life,

To intend my most prosperous life.

I have Faith in the Law of Attraction

To attract financial prosperity and

Abundance each and every day,

Like a magnet.

I have Faith in the Power of Love

With which I am on the same frequency;

Joyfully attracting all good things to me.

I have Faith that

I am manifesting the beautiful, joyful abundant

Life of my dreams –

37

Right now, Today!

Fear, lack, insecurity have no power over me;

For they are only ideas that can be quieted.

I am all and ever abundant.

I am grateful for this knowledge.

And so it is.

Amen.

Healing

Today and every day,

I am surrounded in protective white light.

I am glowing with abundant

Health, healing, and warmth.

I am enfolded in the sheltering embrace

Of Divine Spirit.

Thoughts of dis-ease do not dwell in my mind.

If these thoughts come knocking,

I send them away,

Grateful in the knowledge that I am

Whole, rejuvenated, and renewed each day.

I see that the Power of Love

Comforts and restores me.

And so it is.

Amen.

Help and Support

I always have

All of the help and support

That I need.

In affirming the presence of Spirit in all beings.

I affirm my own connection

To all beings,

Both in the physical and spiritual realm.

I affirm that Divine Spirit is all around me,

In the air, in the Earth, in all creation.

In me.

Guiders and helpers are always here for me

When I face difficulties or questions that

I cannot answer,

All I need do is ask.

I release thoughts of

Lack, helplessness, and

40

Feelings of being overwhelmed;

Embracing all of the good that is here for me now.

Thank you, Sweet Spirit.

Amen.

Answered Prayers

Often when I ask Spirit to answer a prayer,

I am unable to see when it is answered.

Breathing deeply into the awareness of Spirit,

Let me be open to receive help as it comes –

Perhaps in an invitation from a friend,

An unexpected phone call,

Or even canceled plans,

That pave the way for blessings.

I affirm, "My prayers are answered."

In gratitude for this understanding,

Thank you, Divine Spirit.

Amen.

Letting Go

I take a breath and rest in the knowledge

That Spirit lives in me and connects all in my world.

I release fears and tensions, grateful in the knowledge

That Spirit guides me at all times.

All I need to do is let go.

In gratitude,

And so it is.

Amen.

Unity

I affirm that there is one unifying principle,

The Divine Spirit that unites us all and it is good.

I turn my thoughts to love and harmony

As I breathe into this truth.

Divine Love recognizes that there is nothing to fear.

I refute ideas of fear and worry,

Shaking them off like dust.

I am at peace in knowing that

Divine Love is with me at all times.

For this I say thank you God

And so it is.

Amen.

Discernment

I affirm my right and my responsibility

To trust my intuition

In all circumstances.

As I breathe in source energy,

I am gifted with an innate sense of

What is best for me.

I powerfully heed my own ability

To discern the best course to take,

The best choice to make,

The situations, people, and ideas

That I must avoid at all costs.

I do not question myself.

I embrace my duty to trust my gut instincts

I honor the Goddess within by

Heeding her messages for my life.

For the wisdom and guidance that dwell within me

through source,

I am forever grateful.

Thank you, Divine Spirit.

Amen.

Energy

I am an overflowing fountain of energy and vitality.

I am powerful enough to light the world.

When I feel tired, weary, or lazy

I rest.

I go to the water.

I meditate and call forth spirit for inspiration.

I am renewed and I am filled once again to

overflowing

With Divine Energy

I deny lethargy.

I am vibrant, energetic, and powerful.

For this I give abundant gratitude to

Universal Oneness.

Thank You, Thank You, Thank You,

Sweet Loving Spirit.

And so it is.

Amen.

Groundedness

I am grounded.

On Mother Earth.

I am safe, focused, and guided by Spirit.

I have everything I need to live a magical life.

When I feel fearful, I step barefoot onto Mother Gaia

and repeat these words

I am grounded.

Thank you, Mother Earth.

I am focused.

Thank you, Universal Mind.

I am loved and guided.

Thank you, Spirit

All this, I have at all times.

I am grounded, grateful, and filled with love for

myself, my planet and all beings.

And so it is.

Amen.

Creativity

Divine Ideas come to me with ease and grace.

I am open to creative genius.

My mind is a garden,

Ripe with beautiful ideas that dangle and

Sparkle in the light,

Covered in stardust,

Ready to drop from the tree of imagination.

When I struggle.

When I feel blank or empty.

I sit in the stillness. I recede into the water.

I remain open to receive.

I deny any idea that stifles creation.

Affirming that I was born to create

And will do so forever.

Thank you, Universal Creator.

And so it is. Amen.

Connection

I am infinitely connected to Universal Mind.

I am an eternal light being,

Having lived many lives.

Having travelled across the universe.

I have community.

I am community.

I hold connection.

I am connection.

I reach out lovingly in all my interactions

And I am rewarded with love in return.

The idea of alone is false.

For I am never alone.

I am forever connected to Divine Oneness.

I embrace this oneness with joy and gratitude.

And so it is.

Amen.

Community

I live in Community.

I embrace the Oneness of all Life.

When I feel lonely, universal love,

Universal community

Gives me a gentle nudge,

In a call from a friend,

A card from a family member,

A text message, a prayer, a smile.

I am reminded that I live in Community

No matter where I travel

I am always loved, embraced, and enfolded

In Divine Community of Spirit.

For this I hold deep gratitude

Thank you, Sweet Spirit.

And so it is.

Amen.

Confidence

I am bright, bold, and confident,

A sparkling, shining light for all to see!

I radiate confidence

In all that I think, say, and do.

No one can dim my light,

Because I am a majestic and powerful goddess!

A Resplendent Woman!

My confidence comes from the Divinity inside me

Of me and of God.

My energy is renewed by the constant flow of

Light, power, and joy

Which I joyfully receive.

And so it is.

Amen.

Home

I bless my home and all who dwell inside it.

I bless each of my belongings in gratitude.

I honor each room in my home.

I treasure the moments that I have in my home,

Either in peace and quiet,

Or with friends and family

I lovingly send a prayer for my home,

That it be strong, safe, and cared for

As it cares for me and all who cross its threshold.

I have boundless gratitude for my beautiful, lived in,

Well-loved,

Sturdy home.

Thank you, God

Amen.

Gratitude

I am so grateful

I live in gratitude

For all that I have experienced,

All that I have both material and spiritual

All that I can become.

I am a divine being

Of light, love, and understanding.

When I am feeling sad, lacking, and thankless

I look within

I go to nature and behold this resplendent Earth.

I gaze at the azure sky.

I take joy in the sunbeams on the water.

I delight in the calls of the birds.

I am grounded on my planet and in my eternal

Gratitude

For all that I have.

And so it is.

Amen.

Fertility

I am a creative being

My body, mind, and spirit

Are fertile ground for creation.

As source flows through me like a mountain spring,

I am renewed with life,

Love, fulfillment, and possibility.

I powerfully deny ideas such as fear, loneliness,

Idleness, and missed chances,

For these are just thoughts

I can send them away as easily as I call them forth.

I am grateful for my creative power.

I am in awe of my creative power.

Thank you, sweet spirit.

And so it is.

Amen.

Family

Family is a gift from the heavens in so many ways.

Family can be love, care, and trust.

Family may be encouragement, support, and coaching

Family may be guidance, advice, and leadership.

Family can be community, belonging, and

A soft place to land when life is hard.

Or

Family can be disappointing, hurtful, painful, and sad.

As I think of my family, my unique experience with

My unique family,

I see the gifts that I have received

And continue to receive

Whether painful, or joyous

These gifts have shaped my life and given me lessons

On how to live…

Or how not to live.

57

I am grateful for both.

Thank you, Spirit, for the lessons I've learned from

Family.

And so it is.

Amen.

Focus

When I am feeling scattered, confused, and stressed

I stop.

I breathe.

I may even leave.

I go to a quiet place whether internal or external

And I clear my mind

I remind myself that I am,

We are,

All divine beings.

Spiritual beings having an Earthly experience.

I forgive my lack of focus, my humanness.

I laugh at myself.

I find joy in the silliness of stress, fear, and

frazzlement.

I am one with God, the Universe, the Goddess.

I breathe in once again

And peacefully regain my focus.

In gratitude, I go forward,

A powerful, joyful, clear-minded being.

And so it is.

Amen.

Goal Setting

When I set a goal

I bravely take the necessary steps forward

To achieve it

Eventually.

I do not give up

In pursuit of my goal.

When I feel discouraged

When I lose faith in myself

I am gently reminded that I am spirit.

I am oneness,

Stardust, light, and the ability to manifest any dream

That I can dream.

I persevere. I am steadfast. I am one with my goal,

And I see it in sight.

And so it is.

Amen

Intelligence

The infinite mind power of the universe

flows through me.

I AM divine intelligence.

My mind is sharp as a blade.

Quick as a comet.

And soaks up knowledge like a sponge.

When I feel less than,

When I feel that I am lacking,

I release those false beliefs,

Affirming that I am divine intelligence

Now and always.

I am so grateful for my brilliant mind.

And so it is.

Amen.

Virtue

I am a virtuous person.

The qualities of charity, kindness, and

Fortitude are mine.

Because I am a divine child of the universe,

I am free to claim all good things.

Even if I think I fall short,

Even if I misstep,

Even if I am in pain, or have

Caused pain to someone else.

I forgive my past mistakes.

For my past does not define me now.

I live and express myself as a good and virtuous child

Of light and love.

I am so grateful for this loving realization of my

Inner divinity.

And so it is.

Amen.

Leadership

I am a leader.

I am strong, powerful, and wise.

I confidently give good advice that comes

From my own life experience.

I have walked my road, so that I may

Lead others to their highest good.

I have made mistakes, so that I may

Teach others to avoid the same.

I have cried so that I may show others how to

Laugh at their missteps.

I have stumbled and fallen so that I may catch others.

When I feel weak, powerless, or

If I feel like an imposter,

I shake my head, no

And remind myself of my divine power and ability

To lead competently.

In gratitude for my blessings,

And so it is. Amen.

Joy

I am joy.

I am happiness, fulfillment, and wonder.

I love life and all the abundant blessings it brings.

I love the grass, the trees, the sky, the water, and all of

Divine creation.

My joy is fueled each day by my gratitude for all that

I am and all that I have.

Ideas such as sadness, misery, and loneliness have no

Power over me.

For they are simply ideas of the physical mind,

Ideas that I have the power to deny.

I choose joy in my life each day.

And so it is.

Amen.

Health

I am healthy, whole, and perfect.

Through the power of Divine Spirit within me,

All of my trillions of cells are

Rejuvenated, renewed, and restored.

I am free to dismiss ideas such as illness and pain.

And joyfully declare the truth.

That the Universal Spirit of Love

Flows throughout my body,

Giving me perfect health and wholeness.

And for my health, I am so grateful.

And so it is.

Amen.

Fortitude

Today may be a challenge,

But I have fortitude,

I have the courage to forge ahead through pain or

Adversity.

Although my path may seem to be rocky,

I continue on, knowing that I have the strength of

Mind, and firmness of purpose

To prevail.

I am power, divine spirit, and God-given strength,

Goddess-given steadfastness.

In this knowledge, I am grateful.

And so it is.

Amen.

Partnership

I am not alone.

In universal oneness,

I always have a partner.

To share my dreams, aspirations, joys, and sorrows,

I am blessed with partnership, companionship, and

Love.

The idea of loneliness is an illusion.

For I am always connected to spirit, to others,

To all life.

For this divine partnership,

I am forever grateful.

And so it is.

Amen.

Clarity

My thoughts flow

Crystal clear like a mountain spring,

Just as the snow melts on a mountaintop,

Bringing forth a torrent of clean, clear water,

The cells of my brain regenerate and awaken.

My mind is open and

Divine ideas flow freely.

When I doubt my intuition

When I do not trust my inner knowing.

I go into quiet prayer

Denying self-doubt and affirming the

Goddess within.

For my clarity of thought and decision

I am forever grateful.

And so it is.

Amen.

Attunement

I am attuned to my own divinity.

With a deep inner knowing, I affirm that

I am aware and alert,

Tuned into spirit, universal oneness, divine source.

I am one with all.

I feel my spiritual connections to the earth, the stars,

And all life.

When I feel separated,

When I cannot hear spirit,

When I am not receiving guidance.

I breathe into the silence and affirm.

I am attuned.

I am one with all.

God is my source and my being.

I hear the wisdom of the Goddess.

And for this I am grateful.

And so it is. Amen.

Receiving

I am open to receive blessings.

I am open to receive all good things.

I am alert and aware of the gifts that the

Universe brings to me

And lays at my feet.

All I need do is gather them up

Into my arms

And say, "Thank you."

In my highest good,

I always have all that I need.

I am grateful for the gifts I receive each day,

Large or small.

I give thanks for all.

And so it is.

Amen.

Friendship

I am so happy to be blessed with good friends.

I am surrounded by

Love, community, and support.

When I feel alone,

I powerfully deny this feeling.

I know that I am one part of the whole.

One part of a million pieces,

All interconnected.

I can never be alone.

I am surrounded by loving friends at all times.

For this I am grateful.

And so it is.

Amen.

Safety

I am safe.

I am loved, protected, and treasured.

Cradled in the arms of Earth Goddess.

Shielded from harm by Mother, Sister, Aunt,

In the protection of Spirit.

A fortress of love surrounds me, enfolds me, and

Embraces me.

When I feel afraid, I am gently reminded,

That fear is a primitive idea.

I have the power to deny ideas and claim the truth.

That I am always safe, always loved, always cherished.

And for this I am grateful.

And so it is.

Amen.

Ambition

The zealous ambition that I feel for my goals is Divine.

The way that I light up

When I think of my dreams

Is my light from source.

I am created to make my ideas a reality.

I am here, an artist in residence on Mother Earth,

To build, to create, to make, to give birth

To my magical, mystical, divine inspirations.

When I feel discouraged, I take a break.

But I do not give up my dreams.

I simply rest.

And then I return to finish what is mine to do.

For this I am grateful.

And so it is.

Amen.

74

Awareness

I am alive, awake, and aware.

I see with keen eyes all that spirit wants to show me.

When I feel disconnected from the

Flow of divine spirit,

I breathe in new life and as I open my eyes,

I see clearly.

I am grateful for this divine awareness.

And so it is.

Amen.

Kindness

I am kindness.

I give love to my world and all of the people who

Share this world with me.

Sometimes I may feel angry, frustrated, or

Cold-hearted when dealing with others.

I may feel separated from others by

Differing ideas and viewpoints.

I walk away and regroup.

Affirming to myself that we are all connected in spirit.

In gratitude, I realize that there is no separation.

We are in this together.

We are one.

In gratitude, I recognize my divine spirit,

My true nature.

I am loving kindness.

I am love.

And so it is.

Amen.

Compassion

I feel compassion for all life on Earth.

I show compassion in the way I treat others

And in the way I live my life.

I am understanding and forgive of others,

Just as I am,

Forgiving and compassionate to myself.

Knowing that I am, like all beings, a divine expression

of God,

Of Goddess.

I live in grace, humility, and kindness,

Compassionate to all.

And so it is.

Amen.

Open Mind

I am open-minded.

And a seeker of knowledge.

I am adventurous and ready to investigate exciting

New ideas.

I am open to new discoveries,

Knowing what I don't know,

I do not judge what I do not understand.

I put my ego aside and remain open to receive.

Ideas such as fear, prejudice, and moral superiority

Are man-made ideas that I can deny and send away.

In gratitude, I affirm that I am open-minded.

And so it is.

Amen.

Contemplation

Each day, I make time for

Meditation, contemplation, and reflection.

Though I meditate in silence, quieting my mind,

I also take time for contemplation –

To think and to ponder,

To allow divine ideas to come to me.

When I am overloaded with

Chatter, social media, and technology,

Divine guidance is blocked.

In order to tap into source,

I must unplug and go into my silent time.

I do this each and every day, knowing the importance

Of connecting to source.

In gratitude, I receive universal flow of ideas.

And I say thank you, God.

Thank you, Goddess.

And so it. Amen.

Freedom

I am free.

I am a free spirit,

A divine being, universal light.

No one can make me think, do, or believe anything,

Without my participation, agreement, and consent.

I make my own decisions.

My mind is always free to say yes or no.

I always have a choice in every situation.

I am grateful for my freedom to choose.

And so it is.

Amen.

Boldness

I shine my light joyfully, bravely, boldly

For the world to see.

When I am unapologetically bold and powerful,

I am a Resplendent Woman,

Majestic, strong, and awe-inspiring.

I create change for the better.

I lead by example.

I sparkle!

Although I love my light,

My light is also for others to see.

Through my boldness,

I give them permission to shine as well.

Like a beacon, I shine my light boldly,

Inviting others to join in.

Even in small ways, I make an impact on my world.

My boldness matters.

I matter.

And for this I am grateful.

And so it is.

Amen.

Fun

Life is meant to be fun

And I am meant to have fun.

I AM fun.

The Goddess is mirth, silliness, and revelry.

Each day, I take time out to be light-hearted,

To be carefree, and to have fun.

I make plans in advance, affirming that

Fun is part of a balanced life.

I can and should laugh and be joyous.

When I feel guilty about having fun,

I see divine spirit as gleeful, effervescent laughter.

I see myself as a happy, laughing

Divine Goddess.

I am so grateful for fun!

And so it is.

Amen.

Bravery

I am a brave and courageous child

Of the Goddess.

I have fortitude, grit, and strength

To face my task head-on.

I face challenges with wisdom, power, and

Steadfastness.

When I feel fearful, weak, and powerless…

Spirit gently taps me on the shoulder.

Spirit whispers,

"You are Warrior Goddess, strong and sure.

You are Divine Mother, protector of

Women, children, and the elderly.

You are Majestic, Bold, and Wise."

I am reminded to claim my bravery,

Claim my Warrior Goddess self.

I stand firm,

Grounded in Faith

And give thanks for my Warrior Goddess Spirit.

In Gratitude, so it is.

Thank you,

Sweet Spirit.

Amen.

Perception

I am the Power of Perception.

I see,

I hear,

I feel.

And I trust my inner knowing.

I am attuned to my mind and body.

I notice.

I am aware of subtle changes

In my heartbeat.

I feel my gut reaction.

I am the Goddess Freya, Divine Seer.

Armed with the gift of insight.

I get chills.

I experience a certain feeling.

And I know.

My Power of Perception

Is good and trustworthy.

I heed its warnings and its encouragement.

For this power, I am grateful

Thank you, Goddess

Amen.

Capable

I am capable of doing all that is mine to do.

I am able to work hard,

Learn more,

Achieve my dreams.

I am adept and clever.

I am the Goddess Athena,

Pushing forward on my Divine Path.

I am strong, successful, talented, and competent.

When I am feeling less than,

Unworthy,

Or like an imposter,

I envision myself as Athena

Strong and sure,

I cut down my doubts with my blade of truth.

I am grateful that I am capable.

And so it is.

Amen.

Resilience

I am resilient.

Although I may have missteps.

I may stumble.

I may even fall down.

I face my fears

I work through challenges

And I maintain my resolve.

For I am resilient,

Born again from

Past hurts

Mistakes

Regrets.

Like a Phoenix from the flame,

Rises out of the ashes,

I get up and I fly.

Onward and upward, I soar.

New heights, new love, new life

Awaits me.

And I say YES!

Thank you.

And so it is.

Attraction

The Law of Attraction

Is universal law,

Is oneness

Is me.

As I hold thoughts in my mind,

These thoughts have the potential,

To be transformed,

To become things.

In this knowing,

I strive to keep my thoughts

Honest, good, and pure.

I envision

Love, health, happiness, and peace

For planet Earth

And all who dwell on her lands and seas.

I envision

Clear blue water,

Crisp clean air,

Fertile vibrant soil,

Lush green forests,

Fragrant steamy jungles

A land of plenty for all

No lack

No poverty

No disease.

For these are manmade ideas

That I have the power to deny.

I envision

Mother Earth in her perfection

As Gaia is meant to be.

And through the Law of Attraction.

I bring this reality to me.

And so it is.

Amen.

Inspiration

I am Divine Inspiration.

I am galvanized, motivated, and energized

With Imagination and Creative Energy!

When I feel that I am blocked,

Or that my mind is blank,

When I feel uninspired,

I go to nature

I go to the woods

I go to the water

I go to the mountains

I sit in silent meditation.

As I take in my surroundings,

Good ideas flow through me

Like an endless river.

I am invigorated.

My creative light is reignited.

As I affirm,

In Gratitude

I AM Inspired.

And so it is.

Amen.

Caregiver

I am Caregiver,

Nurturing spirit,

Gentle hand to hold.

I am a shoulder to cry on,

A hearty warm embrace

A soft bosom, pillowy arms, and bright smile.

I am reassurance, compassion, and safety.

I am Goddess Kuan Yin.

Divine Mother,

Loving and Compassionate

Caring for the sick, the weak, the saddened.

And when your listless mood

Envelopes you in gray clouds and tears.

I will be present for you.

I will stroke your hair.

And kiss your forehead,

Straighten your blankets,

And bring you tea.

For I am Caregiver.

I AM Love.

And so it is.

Boundaries

I am a loving, friendly, and compassionate soul.

I am warm, cheerful, and funny,

And I have boundaries.

Boundaries give me space,

And time to recharge

And renew my spirit.

I unapologetically observe and fiercely protect

My Boundaries.

I care for myself.

I rest when I feel tired.

I say, "No," when I need to say "No."

I say "No," when I want to say "No."

If an invitation does not feel right,

Or I need space to regroup,

I take what I need.

I do what I want to do without obligations.

I matter.

My boundaries matter.

Saying "No," is my right and indeed,

My duty to the Divine Goddess,

The point of power, the stardust, the magical being

That I am.

I lovingly care for myself with gratitude.

And so it is.

Amen.

Instincts

I value and trust my instincts.

Sometimes, I get a feeling

That I should

Or should not

Do something,

Reach out to a particular person,

Apply for a job,

Or experiment with a new opportunity.

My inner guidance gives me a nudge.

I am receiving

Taps on the shoulder from Divine Spirit,

From the Goddess Within.

So I listen.

I trust.

I never ignore my instincts,

because I have them for a very good reason –

Self-preservation.

Divine knowledge from ancestors, karma, and

Goddesses.

In gratitude, I heed my inner knowing.

And so it is.

Amen.

Patience

I am patient.

I am calm, tranquil, and kind.

I am the Goddess Eir,

Serenely appraising each circumstance.

In taking stock before taking action,

I use divine wisdom and good judgment

And make well-thought decisions

Rather than responding rashly.

It is not my job to teach lessons to total strangers

Based on my own opinions of what is right.

It is not my job to point out flaws in others.

When I feel frustrated, tense, or annoyed

I breathe deeply,

In and out,

Reciting the mantra,

"My Spirit is Divine Spirit

I hold love for all

in my heart

For we are all sparks of the Divine."

Peace floods my soul.

I allow tranquility to enfold me,

Cooling my hot temper

And calming my agitation.

In love and gratitude,

So it is.

Amen.

Resourceful

I am resourceful.

As a child of light, my inheritance is

The Creativity of an artist

The Practicality of my grandmother

The Action of a leader

The Adventurist spirit of an explorer

The Enterprise of an entrepreneur

The Inventiveness of a wild, free-range child

And genius.

Yes, genius.

I am innovative, able, and bright.

I use my talents for my highest good,

New, and exciting ideas bubble from my sharp and

active mind.

When others ask me to dim my light with their words

or their actions,

I do not shrink.

No.

I stand firm in my self-assurance asking,

'Am I honoring the Goddess within?'

And I answer boldly,

'Yes, I Am!'

And so it is.

Amen.

Wise

I am wise.

For I have gathered and stored

Lifetimes of wisdom.

This knowledge is in me, a part of my very being,

My DNA

And my spirit is eternal,

One with all Wisdom

I pay attention

I remain present

I listen

I watch

I learn.

And greater

Becomes my wisdom.

I am daughter, divine mother,

Grandmother,

Wise and respected village Crone.

I share my wisdom

With those who ask

With those who, like me

Are seekers

I in sharing my wisdom,

I help those who are lost

To find their way

In gratitude

I share this gift.

And so it is.

Amen.

Deserving

I am deserving

Of All Good Things.

As a light being

A child of God

Daughter of the Goddess

Diving Being

Miracle.

I am deserving of the blessings that life offers me.

I deserve happiness.

I deserve good health.

I deserve passion.

I deserve a zesty and vibrant life.

I deserve an abundant table and bank account.

I deserve to love and be loved.

I deserve to live my truth and no one else's

I deserve to acknowledge and express my divinity

For the truth is…

I am light

I am love

I am a divine miracle

When I feel sad, sick, lazy, impoverished, or imposter-

ish

Divine Mother reminds me

To be as I am

Divine Spirit of all expressing as me

As only I can do

I am so grateful for this truth

And so it is.

Amen.

I Am Loved

Why am I here?

To love and be loved.

What do I truly want?

To love and be loved.

As a child of Spirit,

I AM love.

I cannot be anything else.

Although at times I may try to hide my true essence.

Spirit knows.

Source knows.

Goddess knows.

God knows.

That I am a being of light and love.

The one power of all,

The power of love

Lives in me,

Fills me

Builds my body

And sustains me.

I am love and I am loved.

So… so very much.

I know this and therefore affirm it,

Thank you, Sweet Spirit.

And so it is,

Amen.

I Am Enough

I am Enough.

It is not my job to be everything to everyone.

I gently remind myself of this truth.

And when I fall short of my own expectations,

I lovingly forgive myself,

For regardless of my years on Earth,

I am still a child,

Offspring of God.

Moonchild of the Goddess.

Daughter of Divine Universe,

Stardust, unbounded love, and curiosity are my

Birthright.

I pick myself up,

And with renewed inquisitiveness,

I continue my journey of learning.

And of joy and love for myself.

In gratitude for all that is

And all that I am

For I am Enough.

Amen.

The Goddess Within

I lovingly honor The Goddess Within.

I am a spark, a point of power, a divine light

I am The Goddess expressing and experiencing

As me.

Through me.

In me.

I am Lakshmi and the Power of Faith.

I am Kali and the Power of Strength.

I am the Wise Sophia.

I am the Loving Compassion of Kuan Yin.

I am the Powerful Isis.

I am the Imagination & Creativity of Saraswati.

I am Concordia and the Power of Understanding.

My Will is steadfast as is Ishtar.

I follow my Divine Path with the Law of Ma'at

I am Pele, passionate in pursuit of my dreams.

Through Tlazolteotl I honor, let go, and

Release that which does not serve me.

I am Life and the Power of Yemaya.

I am grateful for The Goddess Within.

I AM!

And so it is.

Acknowledgements

Special thanks to Bev Spivey and Lawrence Palmer, co-ministers at my spiritual home, Unity of Pompano. Thanks to the beautiful goddesses of Women of Unity, UUWomenSpirit, and The Goddess Tribe. Thanks to Ron Smith and Chris Hanlon for your encouragement. Many thanks to Rhonda (Clower) Bird, Jennifer Ferren, and Jan Kinder. Thank you, Cecilia Lewis and Barbara Jannetta for asking me to write a book of affirmative prayers (so that you don't have to!). Thank you, Nik for being supportive of my dreams.

About the Author

Reverend Radiance Satterfield is an Author, Interfaith Minister, and Spiritual Empowerment Coach. She holds degrees in Computer Information Systems, Communication, and Metaphysics, blending spiritual coaching with business and women's empowerment consulting. She has attended Vanderbilt University, University of Sedona, and University of North Alabama.

After spending years in the corporate world, Radiance has found balance in running her own marketing firm, Aqua Creative Marketing, where she is free to enjoy a spirit-filled life in the digital age. Leading retreats and workshops inspired by her novel, The Goddess Tribe to groups across the USA keeps her busy and brings her joy, as she is continuously in awe of the power of an awakening individual. In her downtime, Radiance loves celebrating her Southern heritage by sharing meals cooked southern style for friends and family. Being outdoors always reminds her of the depth of our connection with the natural world.

Radiance is a certified Life Coach through the Academy of Modern Applied Psychology and is a certified Reiki Master through The ICRT Reiki Membership Association. Radiance has written 2 books- The Goddess Tribe, a novel and Affirmations from The Goddess Tribe.

Radiance has written 2 books,
The Goddess Tribe, a novel and
Affirmations from The Goddess Tribe.

Follow Radiance on the web:
https://www.facebook.com/RadianceCoach/
https://www.instagram.com/ray_dee_ance/
https://twitter.com/radiance_coach
https://radiancesatterfield.com